CW01650210

WHAT A HOOT!

KIDS' JOKES FROM THE NET

From the team who brought you *What a Joke!*, *What a Giggle!* and *What a Laugh!* here's a brand new collection chock-a-block full of fishy jokes, Christmas jokes, spooky jokes, and many others to share with your friends and family. Much-loved illustrator, Terry Denton, adds his own brand of humour guaranteed to make you laugh your head off.

Also by

Phillip Adams and Patrice Newell

What a Joke!

What a Giggle!

What a Laugh!

WHAT A HOOT!

Kids' jokes from the Net

Collected by
Phillip Adams and Patrice Newell

Illustrated by
Terry Denton

Puffin Books

For Aurora

Puffin Books

Published by the Penguin Group
Penguin Books Australia
250 Camberwell Road
Camberwell, Victoria 3124, Australia
Penguin Books Ltd
80 Strand, London WC2R 0RL, England
Penguin Putnam Inc.
375 Hudson Street, New York, New York 10014, USA
Penguin Books, a division of Pearson Canada
10 Alcorn Avenue, Toronto, Ontario, Canada, M4V 3B2
Penguin Books (N.Z.) Ltd
Cnr Rosedale and Airborne Roads, Albany, Auckland, New Zealand
Penguin Books (South Africa) (Pty) Ltd
24 Sturdee Avenue, Rosebank, Johannesburg 2196, South Africa
Penguin Books India (P) Ltd
11, Community Centre, Panchsheel Park, New Delhi, 110 017, India

First published by Penguin Books Australia, 2003

1 3 5 7 9 10 8 6 4 2

This selection copyright © Phillip Adams and Patrice Newell, 2003
Illustrations copyright © Terry Denton, 2003

The moral right of the authors and illustrator has been asserted

All rights reserved. Without limiting the rights under copyright reserved above, no part of this publication may be reproduced, stored in or introduced into a retrieval system, or transmitted, in any form or by any means (electronic, mechanical, photocopying, recording or otherwise), without the prior written permission of both the copyright owner and the above publisher of this book.

Cover designed by Cathy Larsen, Penguin Design Studio
Text designed by Beth McKinlay
Typeset in Gill Sans and Sassoon by Midland Typesetters, Maryborough, Victoria
Made and printed in Australia by McPherson's Printing Group, Maryborough, Victoria

National Library of Australia
Cataloguing-in-Publication data:

What a hoot! : kids' jokes from the Net.

ISBN 0 14 131072 3.

1. Internet – Juvenile humor. 2. Wit and humor, Juvenile.
I. Denton, Terry, 1950– . II. Adams, Phillip, 1939– .
III. Newell, Patrice, 1956– .

808.882

www.puffin.com.au

CONTENTS

THAT'S NOT FUNNY!
KEEP WALKING, CAT! HEE. HEE.
1001 DOG JOKES

giggle bytes

'I cleaned my computer and now it doesn't work properly.'
'What did you clean it with?'
'Soap and water.'
'Don't you know you're not supposed to touch a computer with water?'
'Oh, it wasn't the water that caused the problem, it was the spin dryer.'

'Does your school computer have a brother?'
'No, but it's got a lot of tran-sisters.'

'Help line.'

'I've just pushed a piece of bacon into my disk drive.'

'Has the computer stopped working?'

'No, but there's a lot of crackling.'

'Mum! Dad's broken my computer.'

'How did he do that?'

'I dropped it on his head.'

'I've been sitting at my computer for hours and haven't seen a single web site.'
'That's because you're supposed to sit facing the screen.'

'Computer help line? Every time I log on to the Seven Dwarves web site my computer screen goes Snow White.'

'If you don't stop tapping away at the keyboard, I'll go crazy.'

'You already have. I stopped using the keyboard an hour ago.'

'I've been on my computer all night!'

'Wouldn't you be more comfortable on a bed like everyone else?'

How do you stop your laptop batteries from running out?

Hide their Reeboks.

'Do you turn on your computer with your left hand or your right hand?'

'My right hand.'

'That's strange. Most people use the On/Off switch.'

'You charged me $2000 for this computer, and you said it would be trouble-free.'

'It is. I charged you $2000 for the computer, but you're getting all this trouble absolutely free!'

'I think I've got a bug in my computer.'

'Does it make a humming noise?'

'Yes.'

'Then it must be a hum bug.'

'Want to buy a pocket computer?'
'No thanks, I already know how many pockets I've got.'

What did one mouse say to the other mouse?
I get a click out of you.

What did the mouse say to the web cam?
'Cheese.'

What do computer experts do on weekends?
'They go for a disk drive.'

What do you get if you cross a laptop with a ballet dancer?
'The Netcracker Suite.'

What do you get when you type www.abcdefghijklmnopqrstuvwxyz.com into your computer?
A sore finger.

'Would you like to buy a second-hand laptop?'
'No thanks. I can only type with one hand.'

'Doctor, doctor, I've spent so long at my PC that I've got double vision.'
'Well, go around with one eye shut.'

'Doctor, doctor, I keep thinking I'm a computer.'
'My goodness, you'd better come to my surgery right away.'
'I can't. My power cable won't reach that far.'

'Doctor, doctor, I feel like I'm part of the Internet.'
'Well, you do look a sight.'

Why do computer teachers never get sick?
Because an apple a day keeps the doctor away.

Teacher: I've been typing on the Internet so much, my right hand's begun to ache.
Doctor: That's just age.
Teacher: But my left hand is just as old and it doesn't ache at all.

'Doctor, doctor, can I have a bottle of Aspirin and a pot of glue?'
'Why?'
'Because I've been at my computer all day and I've got a splitting headache!'

beastly jokes

Aunty Ivy was taking her little niece and nephew around the Taronga Park Zoo. They came to a cage containing a stork – and she told them the legend of the big bird, and how it brought little babies to their mums and dads, and dropped them gently down the chimney.

The kids listened with some embarrassment, and one whispered to the other, 'Do you think we should tell Aunty the truth?'

Two elephants walk off a cliff . . . boom, boom!

What does a frog drink when he's on a diet?
Diet Croke.

How did the cow feel when they sent her an e-mail?
She was over the moon.

Why did the monkey fall out of the tree?
He let go.

Why did the duck stick his leg into the laptop?
He wanted to have web feet.

How do you weigh a whale?
You take it to the whale weigh station.

Why do elephants wear green shoes?
So they can hide in your lawn.

How do wasps send messages?
By *bee-mail.*

How do whales type e-mails?
With their *fish fingers.*

How do skunks like their e-mails?
Scent.

'Last night my dad was driving in the country and hit a cow.'

'Was it a Jersey, a Hereford, or an Angus?'

'He doesn't know. He didn't see the licence plate.'

How do skunks send e-mails?

On their com-phew-ters.

How do sheep sign their e-mails?
Ewes sincerely.

Did you hear the one about the chicken that had its mouth washed out with soap?
It was using fowl language.

'What's black and white and red all over?'
'A newspaper?'
'No, a penguin with sunburn!'

Why did the chicken cross the road?

To prove that he wasn't chicken.

What do frogs play in winter?

Ice hoppy.

Why did the turtle cross the road?
To get to the Shell station.

What do you call a fly with no wings?
A sit.

What day do fish hate the most?
Fry day.

What four letters spell hungry horse?
MTGG.

Why do mice have such tiny Balls?
Because very few mice know how to dance.

Why is it so hard to fool a snake?
Because you can't pull its leg.

Who was the first to have a mobile home?
A tortoise.

Mum opens her fridge and finds a duck sitting inside.
'What are you doing in my fridge?' she asks.
The duck says, 'This is a Westinghouse, isn't it?'
'Yes,' says Mum.
'Well, I'm westing,' says the duck.

What is as big as an elephant but weighs nothing?
The elephant's shadow.

What's black and white, black and white, black and white and red all over?
No, not two newspapers. A couple of skunks fighting over a tomato.

What's white and black and white and black and green?
Two zebras fighting over a cucumber.

'What has four legs, eats hay, has a tail and sees just as well from both ends?'
'I don't know – what?'
'A blind horse.'

HEATING DUCK.

swallow this

A blind man goes to the supermarket, manages to find a trolley and get inside.
He then lets his seeing eye dog take him to the first aisle where he picks up the dog and starts whirling it around his head on its leash. He spins it faster and faster and the whirling dog keeps hitting the shelves and sending cans and packages flying.
'What do you think you're doing?' says the store manager.
'Just having a look around.'

What's the smallest room in the world?
A mushroom.

'Waiter. Waiter! There's a fly in my ice-cream!'
'Sorry, Sir. I didn't know that they'd started their winter Olympics so early this year.'

'I've put a fortune into my girlfriend's face.'
'Why? Have you been paying for plastic surgery?'
'No, for meals in expensive restaurants.'

Magistrate: Order, order, order in the court!
Prisoner: I'll have a Big Mac with medium fries.

'How many people work in this supermarket?'
'Oh, about a quarter of them.'

'Do you know what they call lemons in Western Australia?'
'No, *what?*'
'Lemons.'

'Do you know what raisins are?'
'No, *what?*'
'Worried grapes.'

'Name five things that contain milk.'
'Ice-cream, butter, cheese and two cows.'

Two cockroaches were munching on garbage in an alley when one started to describe a new restaurant.

'I was in it just yesterday,' he said. 'It's so clean. The kitchen is spotless. The floors are gleaming white, there's no dirt anywhere – it's so hygienic the whole place shines.'

'Please,' said the other cockroach, pulling a very unhappy face, 'not while I'm eating.'

A mushroom walked into a club and asked a girl for a dance. She said, 'You have to be joking. You're only a mushroom.' And the mushroom said, 'Oh, come on! I'm really a FUN GUY.'

'Is this milk fresh?'

'Fresh? Two hours ago it was grass!'

Why is an egg like a promise?

It's so easily broken.

Last night I dreamt I ate a giant marshmallow
and when I woke up my pillow was gone.

How do you make a Swiss roll?
Push him down a mountain.

I went to the butcher's yesterday and bet him $50 that he couldn't reach the meat off the top shelf. But he wouldn't bet. He said the steaks were too high.

What happened to the butcher who backed into the mincer?
He got a little behind in his work.

Grandma: You've left all your crusts, Fred. When I was your age I ate every one.

Fred: Do you still like crusts, Grandma?

Grandma: Yes, I do.

Fred: Well, you can have mine.

How do you know when you are getting old?

When the candles cost more than the cake.

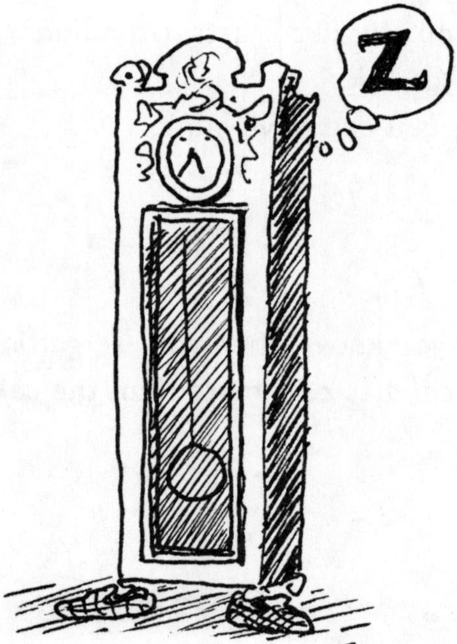

GRANDFATHER CLOCK

Funny families

A kid comes home from school with a black eye. Mum asks what happened.
He says, 'I got into a fight with a kid in my class.'
'That's not very good,' says his mum. 'Give him a chocolate tomorrow and make it up with him.'
The next day the kid returns home with his other eye blackened.
'Now what?' asks his mum.
'He wants another chocolate,' says the kid.

I bought a grandfather clock.
Every half hour it burps and dribbles and then goes back to sleep.

'My dad's cleverer than your dad.'
'No he isn't.'
'Yes he is. I can prove my dad's cleverer than your dad.'
'How?'
'Well, he could have been Prime Minister.'
'Could have been? Then why didn't he take the job?'
'Because if he had there'd be no further chance of promotion.'

'My dad's got a thing in his car that tells him when he's going too slow or too fast and when he's made the wrong turn.'
'Is it one of those satellite guidance systems?'
'No, it's Mum.'

'My mum told Dad that she never wanted to see his face again.'
'What did he say?'
'Nothing. He just stood up and turned out the light.'

There's only one thing that stops your dad from being a bare face liar?
What's that?
His beard.

What kind of person lives the longest?
A rich relative.

'There was a fire in the dunny at my dad's pub last night, and the firemen were there for six hours.'
'Six hours to put out a fire in a dunny?'
'No, it only took them an hour to put out the fire, but it took Dad five hours to put out the firemen.'

'My big sister went on a boat cruise to Vanuatu, and she lost all her clothes.'

'How did she do that?'

'She shoved them all out the round glass door.'

'You mean the porthole?'

'Yep. She thought it was a washing machine.'

Why was the shoe unhappy?

Because his dad was a loafer and his mum was a sneaker.

'My big brother dropped off the eaves of our house and broke his leg.'

'That's what he deserves for eavesdropping.'

'I fell off a huge stepladder today.'

'But you look okay.'

'Yeah, I only fell off the first rung.'

My uncle fell down the stairs. But it didn't matter.

He had to come down anyway.

'My big brother is putting in a huge insurance claim. He reckons he's completely incapacitated by the loss of his thumb.'

'Why, what does he do?'

'He's a professional hitchhiker.'

'How did your dad get that bump on his head?'

'Playing the saxophone.'

'Where was he?'

'In front of the trombone player.'

A man points to a photograph of a baby and says:
'Brothers, sisters have I none.
But this baby's father is my father's son.'
Who is the photo of?
Answer: Himself.

'My mum cut off her thumb when she was slicing bread.'
'I bet she's upset?'
'Yeah, it was the thumb she keeps my dad under.'

Mum: Billy, have you done your jobs?
Billy: What jobs, Mum?
Mum: Well, have you fed the chooks?
Billy: No, I didn't need to. They haven't finished all the seed I gave them yesterday.
Mum: Have you given the goldfish some fresh water?
Billy: No, they still haven't drunk all yesterday's water.

'My brother swallowed a frog.'
'Did it make him sick?'
'Well, he's liable to croak any minute.'

What part of a car causes the most accidents?
The nut that holds the wheel.

'I've got an uncle with teeth like the Ten Commandments.'
'What do you mean?'
'They're all broken.'

'My grandpa's taking us all on a holiday to Amstergosh.'
'Don't you mean Amsterdam?'
'Yes, but my grandpa doesn't approve of swearing.'

Daughter of first film star: How do you like your new dad?

Daughter of second film star: Oh, he's lots of fun.

Daughter of first film star: Yes, isn't he. We had him last year.

'My little brother just swallowed an earthworm.'

'Hadn't you better give him something for it?'

'No. Let the darn thing starve.'

'My mum's got a new baby. It's just three weeks old.'

'What's its name?'

'I don't know. Can't understand a word it says.'

'Under what sign of the zodiac were you born?'
'Under what?'
'Under what sign were you born?'
'It said "St Mary's Maternity Hospital".'

'Where were you born?'
'In Scone. I wanted to be near my mother.'

'Where were you born?'
'I was born on a farm.'
'On a farm? Were there others in the litter?'

'Mummy, you said the baby had your eyes and Daddy's nose, didn't you?'

'*Yes, darling.*'

'Well, he's got Grandpa's teeth too.'

'When I was born I weighed just half a kilo.'

'*Did you live?*'

'Yes. You should see me now!'

'What are your parents' names?'

'*Mum and Dad.*'

'Born?'
'Yes, Sir.'
'Where?'
'Adelaide.'
'What part?'
'All of me.'

'Somebody complimented my mother on her driving today. They left a little note on the windscreen that said "Parking Fine". Mum was very pleased.'

'Does your dad have life insurance?'

'No, just fire insurance. He knows where he's going.'

'Does your dad have an insurance policy?'

'Yes.'

'Accident?'

'No. He took it out on purpose.'

'Mummy! Mummy! Billy broke the window.'

'Oh! Naughty! How could he do that?'

'Well, I threw a rock at him and he dodged.'

Mum was working in the kitchen while listening to Johnny playing with his new electric train set in the living room. To her astonishment she heard him yelling, 'All you louts who want to get off, get off now, because this is the last stop! And all you nerds that are getting on, get your backsides in the train because we're leaving.'

Distressed, Mum went in and told her son, 'You will not use that kind of language in this house. Now, I want you to go into your room for two hours. And when you come out, you can play with your train – provided there's no bad language.'

Two hours later, Johnny came out of his room and continued playing with his train.
'All passengers who are disembarking the train, please remember to take all of your belongings with you. We thank you for riding with us today and hope that your trip was a pleasant one. Please ride with us again soon. Now, for those of you who are just boarding, we ask that you stow all of your hand luggage under the seat, remembering that there is no smoking except in the Club car. We trust you will have a pleasant and relaxing journey with us today . . . And for those who are really cheesed off at the two hour delay, blame Mum.'

I JUST LOVE REINDEER JOKES

yo ho ho!

What do reindeer say before telling you a joke?
This one will sleigh you.

Why do reindeer wear fur coats?
Because they'd look silly in bathers.

If a reindeer lost its tail, where should it go for a new one?
To a retail store.

Which reindeers have the shortest legs?
The smallest ones.

Where do you find reindeer?
That depends on where you left them.

What do reindeer have that no other animal has?
Baby reindeer.

How many legs does a reindeer have?
Six. Forelegs at the front and two at the back.

How long should a reindeer's legs be?
Long enough to reach the ground.

What do reindeer sing to Father Christmas?
Freeze a jolly good fellow.

What do you get when you cross Father Christmas with a detective?
Santa clues.

Why is a reindeer like an apple?
Because they're both green, except for the reindeer.

What do you get when you clap Father Christmas?
Santa plause.

Who delivers presents to baby sharks at Christmas?
Santa Jaws.

Twinkle, twinkle chocolate bar
Santa drives a rusty car.
Press the start, press the choke
Off he goes in a cloud of smoke.

Sick Jokes

What time is it when you have to go to the dentist?
Tooth hurty.

'Doctor, I've got a really bad pain in my right leg.'
'I'm sorry to say that there's no cure for that. It's because of old age.'
'That doesn't make sense, doctor. My right leg is just as old and it doesn't hurt at all.'

Why did the man wear a Gladwrap shirt?
Because the doctor told him to watch his stomach.

A bloke walks into a psychiatrist's office and says, 'I need your help. I'm desperate. You see, I'm convinced that I'm a dog.'
And the psychiatrist says, 'Well, get on the couch and we'll see if we can help.'
And the bloke says, 'Sorry, I'm not allowed on the couch.'

Why did the man have the dentist pull out all his teeth?
So he could chew his gum.

Where do you send a sick ship?
To the dock.

'I'm homesick.'
'Isn't this your home?'
'Yes, but I'm sick of it.'

'My big sister's got another mouth to feed.'
'You don't mean to tell me that she's had a baby?'
'No, she's got a tapeworm.'

'Doctor, doctor! I keep thinking I'm a frog.'
'What's wrong with that?'
'I think I'm going to croak.'

'I don't feel very well today.'
'Homesick?'
'No, I'm heresick.'

A bloke rushes into a doctor's surgery screaming, 'I've just swallowed a billiard ball.'
'I'm sorry,' says the doctor, 'but you'll have to sit on the end of the queue.'

'Doctor, doctor! I think I'm turning into curtains.'
'For heaven's sake man, pull yourself together!'

'Doctor, doctor! I think I'm a butterfly.'
'Will you say what you mean and stop flitting about!'

'Doctor, doctor! I've broken my arm in two places.'
'Well, don't go back there again then!'

'Doctor, doctor! I keep thinking I'm a spider.'
'What a web of lies.'

'Doctor, doctor! I keep thinking I'm a nit.'
'Will you get out of my hair.'

'Doctor, doctor! I keep thinking I'm a bee.'
'Buzz off. Can't you see I'm busy.'

anything goes

Three tourists were crossing the Nullarbor in a car. An American, a Mexican and a Russian. When the car broke down, each man took something. The American took an umbrella, the Mexican a bottle of wine and the Russian a car door. A few days later somebody pulled over to help them.
He asked the American why he had an umbrella – and he said, 'To shade the sun.'
He asked the Mexican why he had a bottle of wine – and he said, 'In case I get thirsty.'
Then he asked the Russian why he was carrying something as heavy as the car door – and he said, 'Well, if it gets too hot, I can just roll down the window.'

What question can you never say 'yes' to?
'Are you asleep?'

'Do you say your prayers every night?'
'No, some nights I don't want anything.'

'If the boss doesn't take back what he said to me, I'm going to leave!'
'What did he say?'
'You're fired!'

'What's the difference between a jeweller and a jailer?'
'I don't know. What's the difference?'
'One sells watches and the other watches cells.'

'What's shaped like a finger, the same colour as a finger and the same size as a finger?'
'I don't know. What is it?'
'A thumb.'

Break the code on this message:
YYUR YYUB
ICUR YY4Me
The translation:
Too wise you are, too wise you be.
I see you are too wise for me.

'These marks on my nose,' said the minister, 'were made by glasses.'

'How many glasses?'

Policeman: Miss, you were doing 120 kilometres an hour.

Driver: Isn't that marvellous! I only learnt to drive yesterday.

'Taxi! Taxi!'

'Were you calling me?'

'Yes.'

'Sorry, I'm already engaged.'

'Oh, are you? Well, I hope you'll be very happy.'

'What are you doing, Jason?'

'I'm writing my girlfriend a letter.'

'But, you can't write.'

'That doesn't matter. She can't read.'

'I see strength, kindness and courage in your face.'

'How can you see all that in my face?'

'I can read between the lines.'

If you were locked in a room with no way out and you saw a piano, a saw, a table and a cricket bat, how could you escape?
You could take a key from the piano and open the door.
You could take the bat and get three strikes. Then you'd be out.
Or you could take the saw and cut the table in two. By putting the two halves together, you'd have a 'whole', and you could crawl through it.

A magician walks down the street *and turns into a bar.*

Why shouldn't you play hide and seek with a mountain?
Because it peeks.

What's lighter than a feather yet the strongest man in the world can't pick it up?
Air.

I went to buy some camouflage trousers the other day, but I couldn't find any.

A woman had a one storey pink house. Everything was pink. The kitchen was pink, the couch was pink. Even the TV was pink. What colour were the stairs?

There aren't any stairs in a one storey house.

What did the tie say to the hat?
You go on a head and I'll hang around.

What's green and smells like paint?
Green paint.

What's brown and sticky?
A stick.

How far can you walk into the jungle?
Half way. After that you're walking out.

What has a head and a tail but no body?
A coin.

What's the best kind of car to drive after summer?
An autumn-mobile.

What goes all around Australia, twists and turns, but never moves?
The road.

What did the careless trapeze artist say?
Catch you later.

How did the giant's wife know that Jack was coming?
She could hear Jack and the beans talk.

What occurs once in a minute, twice in a moment but never in a thousand years?
The letter 'm'.

What weighs nothing, can be seen by the naked eye and makes a barrel lighter if you put it in a barrel?
A hole.

How do you clean a tuba?
With a tuba toothpaste.

Magistrate: Have you a lawyer?
Prisoner: No, but I've got a couple of good mates on the jury.

'I'm looking for new faces!'
'Well, don't look at me – I've had this one for years.'

'How do you feel?'
'I feel just like I look.'
'Oh, you poor thing.'

'Look at this horrible, ghastly, hideous painting.'
'That's not a painting. You're looking in a mirror.'

It's a good idea to keep your words soft and sweet *because you never know when you'll have to eat them.*

You'll never get rid of a bad temper *by losing it!*

If at first you don't succeed *you're about normal.*

Experience is something you never have *until just after you need it.*

When you're in deep water
it's a good idea to keep your mouth shut!

Germs attack people where they're weakest
which is why there are so many head colds.

Most people don't act stupid
it's the real thing!

'My girlfriend's really, really clever. She's got enough brains for two.'
'Then she's the right girl for you!'

'You're a low-down, spineless jelly fish. And you know what I'm going to do to you?

'I'm going to break every bone in your body.'

'Can you tell by his face if he's lying?'

'Yes. When his lips are moving.'

What's square, sits in a corner but goes all around the planet?
A stamp.

Why do farts smell?
For the benefit of those who didn't hear them.

What's big and red and lies in the gutter?
A dead London bus.

Why shouldn't you tell a secret near a clock?
Because time will tell.

What do you call a bell wearing a tutu?
A bellerina.

'Is that the fire brigade?'
'Yes.'
'Well, I've just had a new rock garden built and I've put in some new plants.'
'Where's the fire?'
'And some of these new plants are very expensive and . . .'
'Look, this is the fire brigade. You want the plant nursery.'
'No, I don't. I was coming to that in a minute. My neighbour's house is on fire, but I don't want your firemen running all over my garden when you arrive.'

3
2
1
A
B

What's NEW?

'My dad's got a new invention. It's going to make us millions!'

'What is it?'

'It's hollow soap. It entirely eliminates the useless little leftover bits when we've been using it.'

'My dad's got a new invention. It's shaped like a tractor, is the same size as a tractor and looks like a tractor. Do you know what it is?'

'No idea.'

'A tractor.'

'My dad's got a new invention. He makes shoes out of old banana skins.'

'What kind of shoes could you make out of banana skins?'

'Slippers.'

'My dad has invented a new coffin. It fits over your head like a helmet.'

'What's the idea?'

'It's for people who are dead from the neck up.'

'My dad has got a new invention. It's going to make us a lot of money.'
'What is it?'
'A sauna for chickens. After they've been in there ten minutes they'll lay hard-boiled eggs.'

'Look at this! I've just invented spaghetti!'
'Wherever did you get that idea?'
'Out of my noodle.'

'My dad crossed a kangaroo with a mink. Now he's getting fur coats with pockets. Next he's going to cross a chicken with an octopus so there'll be enough legs to go round.'

what else is new?

Glow-in-the-dark sunglasses.

Waterproof towels.

A book on how to read.

Inflatable dartboards.

Solar-powered flashlights.

A tape on how to put together a VCR.

Powdered water.

Pedal-powered wheelchairs.

WHAT'S A DILL?
ABB

What a dill

A dill joins the airforce. He's given a second-hand parachute and told not to open it until the last minute, because, being second-hand, it's not a good idea to put too much strain on the parachute.

'How long should I wait?' asked the dill.

'Until you're about three metres from the ground,' says the instructor.

'But what if my parachute doesn't open?' asked the dill.

'No problem. Even a dill should be able to jump from three metres.'

Why did the dill think he was upside down?
Because his feet smelt and his nose ran.

Why did the dill cut off his arms?
So he could wear a sleeveless sweater.

Why did the dill leave the bus backwards?
Because he heard someone say they'd grab his seat when he got off.

Why didn't the dill pay his bus fare?
Because his name was Crime, and crime doesn't pay.

Why did the dill go into the living room?
Because he thought he was dying.

Why did the dill cut off his fingers?
So he could write shorthand.

Why wouldn't the dill go out with his wife?
Because he discovered she was married.

What do you call a dill with a wobbly head?
Bob.

Did you hear about the dill buried at sea?
Five dill friends drowned digging the grave.

Why did the dill poke his eyes out?
So he could go on a blind date.

What do you call a dill with one leg?
Eileen.

How do you confuse a dill on the back of a motorbike?
Ask him to wind up the window.

How do you keep a dill busy all day?
Give him a piece of paper with PTO written on both sides.

What happens when a dill does tap dancing?
He falls in the sink.

A dill goes into a bar. He holds out his hand to the barman and says, 'Here, smell my fingers.'
The barman smells them and says, 'That's disgusting.'
The dill asks 'Why?'
'Because it smells like dog poo.'
'Thank goodness,' says the dill, 'I nearly stepped in it.'

There were three dills in a sinking boat. A genie appeared and gave each one a wish.

The first dill said, 'I wish I was home having dinner with my mum and dad,' and he immediately disappeared.

The second dill said, 'I wish I was at the pictures watching *Lord of the Rings*,' and, instantly, he disappeared.

And the third dill said, 'I feel lonely. I wish I had my mates back.'

WHAT A HOOT!

Pet jokes

'Why are you crying, little boy?'
'Well my little dog died today.'
'Don't cry, little boy. My mother-in-law died yesterday, and you don't see me crying like you are.'
'But you didn't raise your mother-in-law from a pup.'

What does a puppy say when he sits on sandpaper?
Ruff, ruff!

Day number 180

8.00am	Oh boy! Dog food! My favourite!
9.30am	Oh boy! A car ride! My favourite!
9.40am	Oh boy! A walk! My favourite!
10.30am	Oh boy! A car ride! My favourite!
11.30am	Oh boy! Dog food! My favourite!
12.00 noon	Oh boy! The kids! My favourite!
1.00pm	Oh boy! The yard! My favourite!
4.00pm	Oh boy! The kids! My favourite!
5.00pm	Oh boy! Dog food! My favourite!
5.30pm	Oh boy! Mum! My favourite!

Day number 181

8.00am	Oh boy! Dog food! My favourite!
9.30am	Oh boy! A car ride! My favourite!
9.40am	Oh boy! A walk! My favourite!
10.30am	Oh boy! A car ride! My favourite!
11.30am	Oh boy! Dog food! My favourite!
12.00 noon	Oh boy! The kids! My favourite!
1.00pm	Oh boy! The yard! My favourite!
4.00pm	Oh boy! The kids! My favourite!
5.00pm	Oh boy! Dog food! My favourite!
5.30pm	Oh boy! Mum! My favourite!

Day number 182

8.00am	Oh boy! Dog food! My favourite!
9.30am	Oh boy! A car ride! My favourite!
9.40am	Oh boy! A walk! My favourite!
10.30am	Oh boy! A car ride! My favourite!
11.30am	Oh boy! Dog food! My favourite!
12.00 noon	Oh boy! The kids! My favourite!
1.00pm	Oh boy! The yard! My favourite!
1.30pm	Ooooo! Bath. Bummer.
4.00pm	Oh boy! The kids! My favourite!
5.00pm	Oh boy! Dog food! My favourite!
5.30pm	Oh boy! Mum! My favourite!

What colour is a happy kitty?
Purrrrrple!

'My dachshund died.'
'That's sad. What happened?'
'He met his end going around a lamp post.'

Why do dogs hang their tongues out of their mouths?
To balance their tails.

What's the difference between a cat and a comma?
One has claws at the end of its paws.
The other is a pause at the end of a clause.

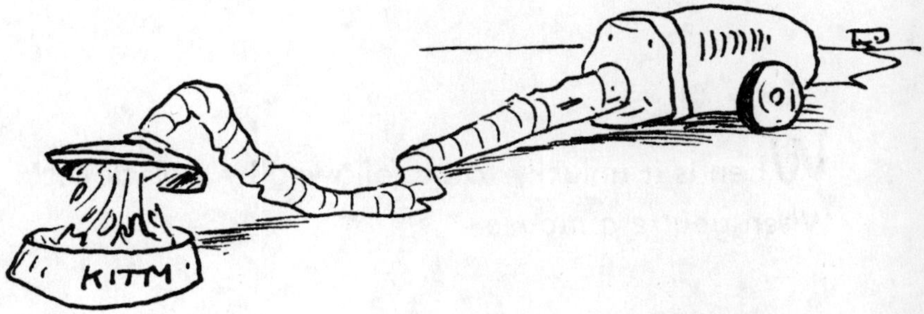

What do you get if you cross a vacuum cleaner with a cat?

Don't know. But it drinks heaps of milk.

Teacher: Class, name five domestic animals.

Class: That's easy, teacher. Two cats and three dogs.

What kind of bike does a dog ride?
A muttercycle.

When is it unlucky to be followed by a black cat?
When you're a mouse.

'Dad! There's a black cat on the kitchen table.'
'Black cats are unlucky!'
'This one isn't. It just ate your dinner.'

'I've got a pet pig. I call him Parker.'

'Is that his real name?'

'No, it's his pen name.'

There are two goldfish in a tank. One says to the other, 'How do you drive this thing?'

Classy laughs

A little boy was sitting in class listening to the teacher talking about the population of the world. 'There are around six billion people living on this planet, and one in five of them is Chinese.'

The little boy turned to the child beside him and said, 'There are five people in my family, so one of them must be Chinese. It's either my mum or my dad. Or my older brother Colin. Or my younger brother Ho-cha Chu. But I think it's probably Colin.'

'Mary, you've been e-mailing other pupils that I'm ugly.'

'Sorry, Miss. I didn't know you wanted to keep it a secret.'

'Johnny, you're not paying attention to me. Are you having trouble hearing?'

'No, teacher. I'm having trouble listening.'

'Sir, would you mind e-mailing my exam results to Mum and Dad?'

'But your parents don't have a computer.'

'Exactly!'

Teacher: Why are you late, Mary?

Mary: Sorry, teacher. I was late leaving home because I slept in.

Teacher: You mean you sleep there, too!

Teacher: Class, we'll only have half a day of school this morning.

Class: Three cheers!

Teacher: We'll have the other half this afternoon.

Teacher: Freddie, why don't you comb your hair?

Freddie: No comb, Miss.

Teacher: Why don't you use your dad's comb?

Freddie: No hair, Miss.

'Billy,' said the teacher, 'where did you get all those nuts and bolts and screws from?'
'From my brother's iron lung,' said Billy.
'And what did your brother have to say about that?'
'Aaaarrrggghhhh . . .!!'

Teacher: Shall I put the school computer on?
Pupil: *No, Miss. The dress you're wearing looks fine.*

'Boo! Boo! Boo!' said the boy.
'What are you doing?' asked his teacher.
'Tomorrow's my big sister's birthday – and I want to surprise her. So I'm practising.'

Teacher: If you want to get ahead, you'll have to work very, very hard.

Student: I've got a head already.

Why is a pencil like a riddle?

Because it's no good without a point!

Little boy: I can't go to school today, Mum.

Mum: Why not?

Little boy: I don't feel well.

Mum: Where don't you feel well?

Little boy: In school!

What did Simon say to the teacher when she asked him to say his name backwards?

'No mis.'

Principal: So you want to be head prefect. Do you ever tell lies?
Student: No, Sir, but I can learn.

Teacher: Did you do this rude drawing on the whiteboard?
Student: No, I didn't.
Teacher: Well, as it happens, I know you did.
Student: Okay, I'm a liar.
Teacher: I don't believe you.

'Where were you born?'
'I was born in Sydney, but I went to school in Brisbane.'
'Gee, that must have been a long ride in the school bus.'

Teacher: Did you tell your child off for imitating me?
Parent: Yep. I told him not to act like a fool.

Teacher: Use the word fascinate in a sentence?
Student: Okay, I've got nine buttons on my sweater, but I can only fasten eight.

Voice on phone: My little boy has a bad cold and won't be able to come to school today.
Teacher: Who is this?
Voice: This is my father speaking.

Dad: How do you like going to school, son?
Son: The going bit is okay. And the coming home bit is okay. But I'm not too keen on the time in between.

Teacher: Why were you late for school this morning?
Pupil: On account of the alarm clock, Sir. Everybody in the house got up except me.
Teacher: Why was that?
Pupil: Well, there are seven of us, and the alarm clock was only set for six.

Three kids were deciding what colour outfits they should wear to the school dance.
The first said, 'My dad's hair is black, so I'm wearing black.'
The second said, 'My dad's hair is white, so I'm going to wear white.'
And the third said, 'I won't be able to go.'
'Why not?' asked his friends.
'Because my dad's bald.'

'What do you call frozen water?'
'Iced water.'
'What do you call frozen ink?'
'Iced ink.'
'You're telling me!'

'Our teacher talks to herself. Does yours?'
'Yes, but she doesn't realise it. She thinks we're listening.'

Student: My mother had triplets, and two weeks later she had twins.
Teacher: That's impossible!
Student: No, it isn't. One of the triplets got lost.

Student: When I was a little boy, I was twins.
Teacher: You were twins? Twins?
Student: Yes, my mother has a picture of me when I was two.

I wanted to call my dog Shakespeare, but the teacher wouldn't let me. She said it would be an insult to the man. So I thought I'd name it after the teacher. But that would be an insult to the dog.

Teacher: This is the fifth day in a row I've had to punish you. What do you have to say for yourself?
Student: I'm glad it's Friday.

Teacher: Why didn't you answer me?
Student: I did! I did! I shook my head.
Teacher: You don't expect me to hear it rattling from here, do you?

Teacher: I'd like to get through one whole day without having to tell you off!
Student: You have my permission.

Teacher: I'm going to give you some problems in arithmetic to see what you've learned. How much is 6 and 4?

Henry: That's about 11, isn't it?

Teacher: No, Henry. 6 and 4 equals 10.

Henry: 6 and 4 can't be 10. That's what 5 and 5 are.

Teacher: Did your parents help you with your homework?

Student: No, I got it wrong myself.

'The brain is a wonderful thing.'

'Why do you say that?'

'Because it starts working the second you wake up in the morning. And doesn't stop until you get asked a question in class.'

'Mary, be sure that you go straight home!'

'I can't, Sir. I live just round the corner.'

Laugh and the class laughs with you.

But you get detention alone.

ONCE UPON a laugh

Teacher: Is there a child in this class clever enough to tell me what the former rulers of Russia were called?

Student: Yes, Sir. I can. Tzars.

Teacher: Correct. And what were their wives called?

Student: Tzarinas!

Teacher: Excellent. And the Tzar's children?

Student: Tzardines!

Why does history keep repeating itself?
Because we weren't listening the first time.

Who succeeded the first Prime Minister of Australia?
The second one.

Teacher: Now, what did Caesar exclaim when Brutus stabbed him?
Student: Ouch!

Teacher: Just think, students, the Great Pyramids are 5000 years old!
Student: You must think I'm really stupid.
Teacher: What do you mean? Don't you believe the pyramids are 5000 years old?
Student: How could they be? It's only 2003.

Who designed Noah's Ark?
An ark-itect.

What was the greatest accomplishment of the early Romans?
Learning to speak Latin.

'Who can tell me where Hadrian's Wall is?'
'Around Hadrian's garden?'

'When was Rome built?'
'At night.'
'Why do you say that?'
'Because my dad says that Rome wasn't built in a day!'

Why did the knight rush about screaming for a can opener?
Because he had a bee in his suit of armour!

Why were the early days of history called the Dark Ages?
Because there were so many knights!

Who invented King Arthur's round table?
Sir Cumference!

What was King Arthur's favourite game?
Knights and crosses!

First Roman soldier: What's the time?
Second Roman soldier: X past VII.

Who invented fractions?
Henry 1/8th!

Why did Henry VIII have so many wives?
He liked to chop and change!

What was Camelot?
The place where people parked their camels!

Why was Camelot famous?
Because of its knight life!

What was the first thing Queen Elizabeth did on ascending the throne?
She sat down!

Where was the Magna Carta signed?
At the bottom!

Why did Robin Hood only rob the rich?
Because the poor didn't have anything worth stealing!

What did the Sheriff of Nottingham say when Robin fired at him?
That was an arrow escape!

'I wish I'd been born a thousand years ago.'
'Why?'
'Then I wouldn't have so much history to learn!'

What kind of lighting did Noah use for the Ark?
Flood lights.

What is a forum?
Two-um plus two-um!

Where did knights learn to kill dragons?
At knight school!

'I wish I'd been born in the Dark Ages.'

'Why?'

'Because I've got pale skin and get terrible sunburn.'

What did Napoleon become when he was 41 years old?

A year older.

Dad: Why aren't you doing better in history, Susie?

Susie: Because the teacher keeps asking me about things that happened before I was born!

Why was the explorer Burke buried in the desert?
Because he was dead!

Do you know the tenth Prime Minister of Australia?
No, we haven't been introduced.

'Henry Lawson had a very difficult childhood. He had to walk seven miles to school every day.'
'Why didn't he get up earlier and catch the school bus like everyone else?'

What does the 1300 BC inscribed on the mummy's tomb indicate?
The rego of the car that ran over him?

NO FISHING.

something fishy

'I know a great place to go fishing.'

'Where?'

'Well, you know that old farm outside the town?'

'Yep.'

'Well, you go down that road for ten minutes and you'll see a place marked "Private". You go through the gate – it has a sign on it saying "Keep Out – Trespassers Prosecuted". Then east of that there's another sign saying "Positively No Fishing".'

'What about it?'

'That's the place.'

'Are you fishing?' the old bloke asked the little boy who was sitting with a rod at the river.

'No,' said the boy, 'I'm just drowning worms.'

What did Noah do to pass time on the Ark?

He fished. But he couldn't catch much.

He only had two worms.

'What kind of fish are they, Dad?'
'They're jellyfish, son.'
'What flavour?'

'Do you know how Eskimos go fishing?'
'No, how?'
'When the water is frozen over with ice, they cut a hole in it. Then they hold a watch over the hole, and when the fish come up to see what time it is, they hit them on the head.'

First pelican: Pretty good fish you've got there.
Second pelican: It'll fill the bill.

What do you call a fish with no eyes?
A fsh.

A fish hits its head on a cement wall.
'Dam.'

If fish aren't happy to be caught, *why do they wag their tails at me when I pull them out of the water?*

'I saw a man-eating shark at the aquarium.'
'That's nothing. I saw a man eating fish and chips on the train.'

What makes the sea salty?
Fish sweat.

'In far north Canada, Eskimos use fish as money.'
'They use fish as money?'
'Yes, when they go to the store they pay in fish.'
'Their ATMs must be really messy.'

but, sir . . .

Two teachers are talking about a student.
'What excuse does Aurora make for not doing her homework?'
'All of them.'

Like . . .

I lost my homework fighting this bully *who said you weren't the best teacher in the school.*

My puppy toilet trained on it.

I put it in a safe but lost the combination.

I left it in my shirt pocket and Mum put it in the washing machine.

Some aliens from outer space borrowed it so they could study how the human brain works.

My little sister ate it.

A kid fell into the swimming pool and I jumped in to save him. And my homework got drowned.

My guinea pigs had babies, and used it to make a nest.

I made a paper plane out of it and it got hijacked.

I didn't do it because I didn't want to add to your already heavy workload.

GOOD SHOT, MERV
VERY SMALL PLANET!

jeepers creepers

'I went to a fortune teller and she read my palm.'
'And what did she tell you?'
'That someone was going to steal my car.'
'But someone stole your car six months ago.'
'I told her that and she said, "I can't help it if you haven't washed your hands for six months." '

What do werewolves put at the bottom of their e-mails?
Beast wishes.

Why don't skeletons send e-mails?
Because they have no body to do it with.

Why do witches fly on brooms?
Because vacuum cleaners are too heavy.

What sweets do ghosts like best?
I-scream with boo-berry pie.

When a knight in armour was killed in battle, what did they carve on his headstone?
Rust in peace!

What side of a monster has the most hair?
The outside.

'What has 24 feet, green eyes and a pink body with purple stripes around it?'
'I don't know – what?'
'I don't know either. But there's one crawling on your shoulder.'

'When Grandpa dies, he's threatened to come back and haunt me. But I'm not scared.'
'Why not?'
'Because he hasn't got a haunting licence.'

'Is it possible to communicate with the dead?'
'Well, I can hear you distinctly.'

'I saw a ghost last night.'
'What did it look like?'
'It looked like an idiot.'
'I think you're afraid of your own shadow.'

'Excuse me, ghost. How much will you charge me to haunt my big brother?'
'For $10 I'll scare him out of his wits.'
'Here's $5.'
'I said $10.'
'Yes, but my brother's only a half wit.'

I hope in your next life you're a centipede and have ingrown toenails.

E-JOKES

Why do church bells never send e-mails?

They'd rather give each other a ring.

Why don't Vikings send e-mails?

They prefer to use Norse code.

Why couldn't the apple send an e-mail to the orange?
Because the lime was engaged.

How do mountaineers send e-mails?
By ski-mail.

Why don't you stamp e-mails?
Because your foot would go right through the computer screen.

How do athletes send e-mails?
On the inter-sweat.

How do long-distance runners send e-mails?
On the sprin-ternet.

Why couldn't the alligator send e-mails on his PC?
Because it was an old croc.

How do pimples send e-mails?
On the skin-ternet.

How do very short people send messages?
By wee-mail.

How do writers send e-mails?
On the ink-ernet.

How does Old MacDonald send messages?
By e-i-e-i-o mail.

How does James Bond type e-mails?
With his Goldfinger.

How does Robin Hood send messages around Sherwood Forest?
By tree mail.

How do animal lovers send e-mails.
On the inter-pet.

'I've been e-mailing Beethoven.'
'Beethoven's dead, you dill.'
'No wonder he hasn't replied.'

'I tried to send an e-mail, but broke my computer.'

'How come?'

'I think it was when I tried to push it through the letterbox.'

'I've lost my puppy.'

'Have you tried putting a message on the Internet?'

'That wouldn't help. My puppy never reads e-mails.'